WILDERNESS SELF RELIANCE

Tracking in its truest form is an art and not something that can be learned quickly or easily. Some simple guidelines can be used to better understand animal behavior and patterns using simple tracking techniques to secure food.

To me, there are three ways of securing food in the wild. They are: hunting, fishing (these include trapping) and foraging. Foraged food (plants) will give you important vitamins, minerals, starches and some protein from nuts, but animal fat and protein from animal sources are an absolute must and can provide nearly 90% of your short-term nutritional needs.

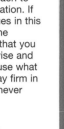

My Pathfinder Outdoor Survival Guides offer a simple and common sense approach to being prepared for any survival situation. If you practice the skills and techniques in this guide, you will be prepared when the occasion arises. Most important is that you develop the ability to adapt, improvise and overcome adversity by learning to use what is available to you. And that you stay firm in your belief that you CAN survive – never give up.

The Pathfinder School System®

Created as a teaching tool for my students in Wilderness Self Reliance, the Pathfinder School System represents the wisdom of the ancient scouts who ventured ahead of nomadic tribes to find fresh areas to support their community.

These "Pathfinders" had to accurately identify the perfect spot to sustain their tribes – they had to recognize the resources that would afford food, shelter, water, medicines and protection – the very same resources a person would need today.

This system is designed to introduce you to the knowledge you need to increase your survivability.

Before You Go

Most survival concepts can be broken into three basic elements (The Pathfinder School 'Rule of 3's'). If you can control these three elements, you will improve your survivability chances:

3 main killers of most lost or stranded people: hypothermia, hyperthermia and shock.

3 ways bodies gain or lose heat: radiation, conduction and convection.

3 basic needs for body function: rest, water and food.

Dave Canterbury is a master woodsman with over 20 years of experience working in many dangerous environments. He has taught survival and survival methods to hundreds of students and professionals in the US and around the world. His common sense approach to survivability is recognized as one of the most effective systems of teaching known today. For information on Pathfinder programs and materials visit http://www.thepathfinderschoolllc.com.

N.B. — The publisher makes no representation or warranties with respect to the accuracy, completeness, correctness or usefulness of this information and specifically disclaims any implied warranties of fitness for a particular purpose. The advice, strategies and/or techniques contained herein may not be suitable for all individuals. The publisher shall not be responsible for any physical harm (up to and including death), loss of profit or other commercial damage. The publisher assumes no liability brought or instituted by individuals or organizations arising out of or relating in any way to the application and/or use of the information, advice and strategies contained herein.

Made in the USA

Waterford Press produces reference guides that introduce novices to nature, science, survival and outdoor recreation. Product information is featured on the website:
www.waterfordpress.com

ISBN 978-1-58355-709-9 $7.95 U.S.

10 9 8 7 6 5 4 3 2 1 206701

Text and illustrations © 2012, 2020 by Waterford Press Inc. All rights reserved. Images marked IC © Iris Canterbury 2012, 2020. For permissions, or to share comments, e-mail editor@waterfordpress.com.

To order or for information on custom-published products, call 800-434-2555 or e-mail info@waterfordpress.com.

BASIC TRACKING – A Waterproof Folding Guide to Familiar Animal Signs in the Eastern Woodlands

PATHFINDER OUTDOOR SURVIVAL GUIDE™

BASIC TRACKING

A Waterproof Folding Guide to Familiar Animal Signs in the Eastern Woodlands

THE PATHFINDER SCHOOL
www.thepathfinderschoolllc.com

TRACKING

In a survival situation where you have taken care of the basics of fire, water and shelter, and have set up every means of signalling at your disposal, then depending on your circumstances and the length of time you have been without nourishment, your next priority is to find a food source.

Tracking is not only the art of following an animal by visual "sign" but also the art of understanding where the animal might be at a given time so you can procure food. To track effectively, you need to be able to see the signs, know what they mean, and be able to predict where your quarry might be in order to find it.

Trackers must be able to recognize and follow animals through their signs and trails, which is also known as spoor. Spoor can include tracks, scat, kills, marking or scratching posts, beds/nests/dens, trails, drag marks, scents, as well as other animals and the habitat you are in. Understanding and interpreting these signs will offer an opportunity to find food, and just as importantly, can help you avoid dangerous predators on their own ground.

Water Is 'Nature's Supermarket'

Aside from the species that live there — such as fish, turtles, crayfish, frogs and snakes, water is the place that most other species will gravitate to at some point to replenish their own hydration.

These are some good signs:

Lily Pads – provide excellent cover for many types of fish. Drop lines around edges of lily pads and through openings between the pads;

Weed Beds (either fully submerged or near the shore) – generally offer fish shelter and food source. Fish the edges or in the beds using non-plant bait;

Submerged Objects – sunken logs, rocks, and trees offer food and shelter – drop lines at different angles to tempt whatever is hiding in the shadows.

Creek Mouths, Points/Steep Shores – usually indicate possible holes or drop-offs where fish can be found.

Tracking Involves the Art of Being Invisible

Animals see patterns and abnormal shapes before they actually see you. Our eyes, faces and hands are often the first thing prey will see, followed by the outline of our bodies. Where you can, cover your face and hands and wear loose-fitting clothing to blend into your surroundings when you are hunting or tracking game. (Don't tie branches to your head and arms – the other thing animals notice is movement, and branches will exaggerate your movements).

TIP All birds are edible and most are catchable either by trap or by weapon. Most mammals are edible, even if you would not want to eat them normally.

TRACKING RULES TO REMEMBER

1. All life needs three things, shelter (cover), water and food

By understanding which type of cover various species use, how and when they seek water, and the types of foods they eat, you will be more easily able to find the animal.

2. Water is a natural food attractant – if the water is not toxic, you are most likely to find food sources nearby

Not only will wildlife come to water, you will find many forms of food in and around the edges of any water source – including amphibians (frogs & toads), reptiles (snakes, terrapins), and fish.

3. Small prey is easier to catch and process than larger meat sources

As with other basic survival activities, remember that the energy you invest to catch your food has to offset the likelihood of actually catching it, and the nutrient reward you will gain. If you are in the right habitat, it is much easier to catch a small mammal than it is to catch a deer, so learn how to identify signs of rabbits, skunks, squirrels, mice/voles and rats.

4. Live food never spoils

A frog or a turtle in a sack does not have to be processed and consumed right away whereas a dead animal on a hot day may spoil if not attended to immediately.

5. Think like the animal you want to catch

You need to know their dominant senses – for some animals, it's their sense of smell, others, hearing, and still others, it is their eyesight. You should know which other animals pose a danger to your prey, so you know what to NOT mimic. Know what sense they will use first in identifying danger and fleeing.

6. Remember animals are attracted by both olfactory and visual stimulation

If you can, mask your own odor by either standing in smoke, which has a natural smell to animals, or crush up fragrant non-toxic plants and rub them on your clothes. Remove any brightly colored garments while you are tracking, if you can; non-solid colors offer the best camouflage.

7. If you can see the animal, chances are he has already seen you

In general, animals have excellent eyesight. They will easily notice the whites of your teeth and eyes, so keep your lips closed and squint your eyes if the animal is standing still. In cold weather, when your breath is more visible, try to direct it along the body so the plumes of air are not obvious.

8. Don't waste anything from an animal after processing, everything is bait

First of all, kill and gut your prey away from your camp/shelter to avoid attracting unwanted predators looking for easy food. Secondly, be sure to save all of the animal waste to use for other bait.

9. Take advantage of travel routes

The best time of day to find animals on travel routes is at dawn and dusk. Staking out a route at one of these times, with appropriate scent masking and camouflage, will greatly increase your chances of finding game.

10. Use opossum mentality

Become a scavenger and seek food at all given opportunities no matter what else you are doing at the time.

TRACKING

How to Track

1. **Walk into the wind** when possible. Mammals have an excellent sense of smell and will leave an area once they pick up your scent.
2. **Move carefully and slowly.** Try to detect motion in the distance, and be aware that animals are watching their surroundings the same way.
3. **Be quiet as you move.** Avoid stepping on twigs. Listen for animals calling to each other or moving through the area.
4. **Recognize animal signals.** Squirrels will go silent when a danger is present, so a sudden hush in the natural sounds should alert you to a foreign presence.
5. **Listen for animals moving** through the bushes. Louder movement suggests a larger animal.
6. **Watch for patterns.** In a stand of trees, you will see a deer first as a horizontal line (its back), or by the movement of its ears or tail twitching.

Basic Tracking Practices

1. **Keep your head up.** Look at signs as far ahead as you can – on trees (branches broken, trunks scratched or gnawed), in bushes and grass (knocked aside or bent).
2. **Look for animal highways.** There will be well-traveled feeding, water and bedding areas connected by worn trails. Depending on the habitat, many species of animals will probably use the same trails as a way to conserve energy.
3. **Recognize beds and other resting areas.** Beds will be well-compacted spots about the size of an animal's body. Some species will change bedding areas frequently; others will keep using the same area as long as they are not aware of any danger and if food and water are nearby.
4. **Rubs and scratching** are evident on tree trunks and branches, and sometimes you will see hoof nicks on fallen logs across a well-traveled trail. These should alert you to animal presence. Be especially aware of hairs or claw marks, which can help to warn you of bears.
5. **Watch for signs of an animal's eating.** Sometimes you will see signs of an animal digging for food – skunks, rodents and even bears will dig at the base of a fallen tree or log for insects and grubs. A pile of pine seeds at the base of a tree suggests squirrels eating above. Browse on grasses or branches can indicate herbivores such as rodents, rabbits and deer.
6. **Animal droppings (scat) are extremely useful signs.** Not only do they tell you what family or species is in the locale, but they tell you what the animal has been eating. Extremely useful information as you try to sustain yourself on the natural flora and fauna.

LANDSCAPE TRACKING

The simplest form of tracking is called Landscape Tracking. Landscape tracking is used to understand what areas of a given habitat are most likely to produce good hunting grounds. Understanding where animals spend time and how they prefer to travel will help you when tracking down places to hunt, trap, and fish. Landscape tracking knowledge includes:

Learning Behavioral Patterns

Animals can be **diurnal** (active during the day), **crepuscular** (active at dawn and dusk) or **nocturnal** (active at night). Knowing the different species' behavioral pattern will help you find them, and will help you know if a behavior is out of character, which could mean that they are sick and possibly toxic as a food source. For instance, finding a raccoon, which is typically nocturnal, walking along a trail in the daylight would suggest it is likely sick and that you should avoid it.

Understand Species' Cover Needs

All animals prefer cover so unless they are watering or feeding that is the most likely place to find them. Keying in on the types of cover animals prefer will also help you to identify possible whereabouts, and cover near food and water sources called "edges" will be excellent areas to look. Rabbits will prefer thick grassy areas that border a meadow, while a squirrel will live in a tree near his food source.

Remember that animals are constantly on the lookout for predators so they are most wary at feeding and watering areas where they are exposed and away from cover.

Recognize Travel Routes

Areas between cover, food sources, and water are called travel routes. Areas around travel routes are great places to hunt and trap. An animal on a mission using a travel route will be less wary with food or water on the brain that when he is already there, making travel routes again the best place for hunting and trapping activities.

Understand Species' Food Sources

Understanding what each type of animal eats or forages will also help you narrow down possible locations of the animal. If you are looking for squirrel, for instance, Oak and Hickory stands would be logical because they are a source of nuts, while a raccoon may prefer foraging around water for crayfish or small fishes and snails.

Water Needs

Animals need water for the very same reasons humans do: to aid digestion, to support biochemical processes, to maintain body temperature and to remove metabolic waste. Different species need different amounts of water and will get their water from a variety of sources. Knowing which species will go to a body of water, rather than getting their fluids from the dew on grasses and other sources will help you be more successful in staking out and catching your prey.

Edges of forests and waterways are great places to trap and hunt as these are the areas where animals will move in and out of cover to forage for themselves leaving the comforts of cover can make animals more alert but will yield a greater visibility and sometimes block an easy escape route in the case of waterways for most mammals.

SIGN TRACKING

Sign tracking is used both to identify what animals are in the area as well as where they have been or where they are going. In the Pathfinder School System we teach seven types of Animal Signs to help you with this process. When combined with Landscape Tracking this will give you needed information to trap and hunt.

1. Tracks
The footprints of an animal left for you to identify. Aging tracks is an art form in itself but there are some simple things you can use to help understand at least if the tracks are fairly fresh.

a. Weathering – Is the track fully intact or does it look worn down from last night's rain, if the track was in fresh snow has it melted some from the midday sun?

b. Dampness – If it is midday and the sun is up or it is windy but the track is visibly wet, even if near a water source, the track is most likely fairly new.

c. Self Timing – Were you here before? If so when? Was the track present then?

2. Scat
Animal scat or feces is another way to identify what animals are in the area, as well as what they are feeding on. It can also give you a timeline when using the rules above for tracks.

3. Slough
These are anything the animal leaves behind naturally during daily activity. It could be a feather from preening, a piece of hair stuck on a tree trunk, or snakes' shed.

4. Refuse
This is the animal's garbage what he leaves behind like nut shells, or a crayfish carapace.

5. Remains
Skeletal remains of animals will give you a clue to at least what animals are in the area and if fresh enough maybe provide bait for trapping or fishing. (Never consume an animal unless you know how and when it died).

6. Disturbance
This is a sign that an animal has been in the area. It could be an eaten or grazed area along a path, a hole dug by a squirrel for nuts, or broken branches along a trail.

7. Dens and Lairs
These are areas specifically designed for animals to sleep or rear young, a typical example would be a fox den in the side of a dirt bank or a small cave, it could even be a hollow log where the nocturnal opossum is sleeping.

8. Smells
Many animals like skunks, weasels and foxes have distinctive smells. Bears smell like rotting garbage.

9. Sounds
Wolves and coyotes howl, elk bugle, marmots and prairie dogs whistle loudly when danger approaches.

SIGN TRACKING

Squirrel Nest

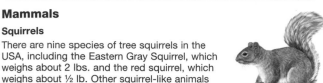

Mouse Nest

Tree Hole

Beaver Lodge

Rodent Burrow

Rabbit Nest

Fox Den

Vole Tunnel

Muskrat Lodge

Rabbit   Porcupine   Deer   Dog/Cat

Browse

Deer Bedding Area

Bear   Deer
Scratch Marks on Trees

Hair

Bird Pellet
Owls, eagles, hawks and ravens often regurgitate pellets of undigestible material.

Chewed Plants
Rodent or deer sign.

MAMMAL SCAT

The size, shape, color and content of droppings (scat) give key information about the animal and its diet. In general, the scats of predators are long and twisted and contain the fur, feathers or bones of its prey. Herbivores have 'pellet-like' or 'pie-like' scat depending on their diet and the time of year.

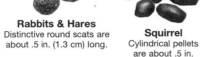 

Rabbits & Hares
Distinctive round scats are about .5 in. (1.3 cm) long.

Squirrel
Cylindrical pellets are about .5 in. (1.3 cm) long.

Mice & Rats
Cylindrical, rice-like scats are between .3 in.-.8 in. (.8-2 in.) long.

 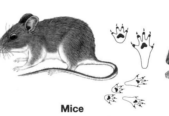

Dog Family
Scat is usually a single cord with a pointed end. Droppings vary greatly in size and diameter and may be up to 5 in. (13 cm) long.

Porcupine
Pellets are about 1 in. (3 cm) long and often collect in huge piles in and around their dens and under trees.

Weasel Family
Scat is usually black and twisted and may be up to 4 in. (10 cm) long. Family members include weasels, minks, skunks, otters and badgers.

Cat Family
Scat is usually segmented and often buried. It varies in size and may be up to 4 in. (10 cm) long.

Deer Family
Distinctive pellet scats are pointed on one end and concave on the other. Scats vary in shape, but are about 1 in. (3 cm) long and deposited in small piles. Droppings are typically pellets in winter and chips or 'pies' in summer. Family members include deer, pronghorns, elk, mountain goats, caribou and bighorn sheep.

Northern River Otter
Scats are up to 7 in. (18 cm) long and .75 in. (2 cm) in diameter. Black when fresh, they are often deposited in piles in conspicuous places along the water's edge. Muskrats have the same behavior.

Moose
Oblong scats are about 1.5 in. (4 cm) long and deposited in large piles. Droppings in summer are loose 'pies'.

Bears
Scats are typically thick (to 2 in./5 cm) and cord-like, with blunt ends. When bears eat primarily vegetation, e.g., during berry season, scats are a loose mass.

TIP If you find scat with berries or a distinguishable food source in it, locate the food source to find clues about the species.

MAMMAL TRACKS

One of the easiest signs to interpret an animal's track is defined by the shape of its feet, its weight, and the way it walks, runs or hops. The size of a track generally indicates the size of the animal. Sandy or muddy soils are the best places to find clear tracks. The best time to look for tracks is following rains, fresh snowfalls, or at dawn when the dew makes tracks easy to identify. Keep in mind that tracks are influenced by several factors including the age and size of the animal, the material it walks on, the season (some mammals grow extra fur between their toes in winter), the age of the track and the animal's stride. Is it walking, loping or running?

The pattern of tracks is also a good indicator of the species. Generally speaking, there are four kinds of track patterns. Deer, dog and cats are diagonal walkers and walk with a front foot and the opposite back foot moving at the same time. Most weasels are bounders and push off with their front feet, have their back feet land near the front feet tracks, and then push off with the back feet. Rabbits and most rodents are gallopers that push off with their back feet and land on their front feet with the front tracks behind the rear tracks. Lastly; raccoons, bears, porcupines and beavers are amblers which move with a front foot and same side back foot moving at the same time.

Mice
Hind track is about .7 in. (1.8 cm) long. Front track shows 4 toes. Tracks in soft soil usually show tail drag between feet.

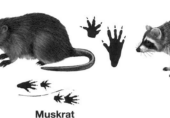

Squirrels & Chipmunks
Hind tracks are 1-2 in. (3-5 cm) long with 5 toes. Front tracks are smaller and show 4 toes.

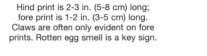

Rabbits & Hares
Rabbits and hares all have rear feet at least twice as long as their front feet.

Ground Squirrels
Hind tracks are 1-2 in. (3-5 cm) in length with 5 long toes.

bound

Opossum
Distinctive, hand-like tracks are about 2 in. (5 cm) wide. Tracks show tail dragging on ground between feet.

MAMMAL TRACKS

Beaver
These animals have webbed feet. Hind tracks are about 6 in. (15 cm) long and the webbing between the toes is often visible in mud.

Skunks
Hind print is 2-3 in. (5-8 cm) long; fore print is 1-2 in. (3-5 cm) long. Claws are often only evident on fore prints. Rotten egg smell is a key sign.

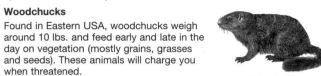

Muskrat
Hind track is about 3 in. (8 cm) long and has 5 toes. Leaves scat in piles near waterline. Look for floating grassy lodges near shore.

Raccoon
Tracks are like small hands. Hind prints are 4 in. (10 cm) long and claws are clearly visible. Hips roll while walking causing the hind foot to register beside the opposite front foot.

Dogs
Dog tracks show claws. The foot pad is small in relation to the toes and has a single lobe. They range in size from 2-5 in. 5/13 cm.

Cats
Cat tracks do not show claws. The foot pad is large in relation to the toes and has two lobes. Note the rounded toe pads. They range in size from 2-4 in. 5/10 cm long.

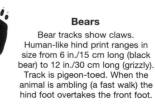

Bears
Bear tracks show claws. Human-like hind print ranges in size from 6 in./15 cm long (black bear) to 12 in./30 cm long (grizzly). Track is pigeon-toed. When the animal is ambling (a fast walk) the hind foot overtakes the front foot.

ANIMALS FOR FOOD

Mammals

Squirrels
There are nine species of tree squirrels in the USA, including the Eastern Gray Squirrel, which weighs about 2 lbs. and the red squirrel, which weighs about ½ lb. Other squirrel-like animals include the Chickaree. Squirrels usually feed on calm days early in the morning and later in the day. If weather is bad, they may try to wait it out and can be found mid-day or later in the afternoon/evening.

Tree squirrels eat nuts, fruit, berries, twigs and bark. You will usually find squirrels among oak, beech, hickory and other nut trees. If you learn to identify these tree species, you will improve your chances of finding squirrels if you need them. Note: if you capture a squirrel, be sure you have stunned or killed it before you pick it up. It can inflict a nasty bite.

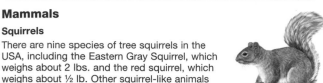

Gray Squirrel

Fox Squirrel

Woodchucks
Found in Eastern USA, woodchucks weigh around 10 lbs. and feed early and late in the day on vegetation (mostly grains, grasses and seeds). These animals will charge you when threatened.

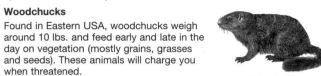

Woodchuck
Also called groundhog.

Muskrat and Beaver
Found near water, best caught with traps. Beavers have a scent-sac that must be removed immediately or it will foul the meat.

Birds
Small birds are best trapped but can be taken with pronged spears or thrown clubs/rocks. Ground birds such as quail, grouse and pheasants can be snared using seeds or grains as bait.

Quail

Fish
Are harder to catch in summer. Food is more plentiful so they get more selective, and cover at the edges of waterways is more abundant, so they are harder to see. Fish activity is affected by water temperature. Trout, pike and salmon like temperatures between 50 and 60 degrees, bass, crappie, walleye, catfish, carp, muskie and perch like temperatures between 65 and 76 degrees. While you won't know the exact temperature of the water around you, knowing what is likely to be found is a help when you are choosing your bait and fishing method. Finding fish in water that has no structure (plants, banks, breaks) is not likely to have fish, so trying to find fish on a sandy bank with shallow water would be unwise.

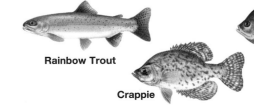

Rainbow Trout

Bluegill

Crappie